I0597030

GET UP

AND

DANCE

Dance Poems

CHARLES D. TARLTON

Get Up and Dance
Dance Poems by Charles D. Tarlton
Cover art by Ann Knickerbocker

ISBN: 978-0-9980375-3-0

Published: September 2019
KYSO Flash Press
Bellingham, Washington, USA
http://www.kysoflash.com

Please send questions and comments to the Publisher at:

KYSOWebmaster@gmail.com

To Ann,

who just danced into my life

Also by Charles D. Tarlton

Touching Fire: New and Selected Ekphrastic Prosimetra
KYSO Flash Press (2018)

Una Vida de Piedra y de Palabra
Number 23 in the 2River Chapbook Series
http://www.2river.org/chapbooks/tarlton/default.html
(May 2010)

Fortune's circle: A Biographical
Interpretation of Niccolo Machiavelli
Quadrangle Books (1970)

Table of Contents

the commonest things
perplex the eye at high speed...

[...]

Artifact With Steam (2019) by Ann Knickerbocker

*This is a revision of my "St. Ives" painting which, although abstract in
form, seemed too realistic. The earth and sea are still in charge,
but the overlays are more passionate here…
the way I feel about "place."*

—Ann Knickerbocker[2]

1

I woke from a nap on the flight back from Dublin to Boston and
looked out the window. We were in thick clouds and I could barely
see the green navigation light at the end of the wing that flickered as
bits of mist raced by in front of it. Thin mist raced over the top of the
wing and disappeared, like the froth from a mountain stream
slipping over the rocks. The steady light from inside the airplane fell
across the wing closer up, while slowly pulsing white light seemed to
come from somewhere underneath the plane. The light from the
passenger windows was reflected in the cloud vapor and made it
seem that the plane was surrounded by something thicker, heavier,

and more mysterious than just clouds. We were in the middle of some matter or force that kept pace with the plane's 600-mile-per-hour speed.

the commonest things
perplex the eye at high speed
short, tall, heavier
lighter, fast and slow, closeup
or far away transfigured

they commonly use
mist or fog in rock concerts
to create something
out of the ordinary
mystical transformations

have you ever seen
football played in viscous fog
the passes come out
of nowhere and disappear
cheers let you know they were caught

2

Take a simple experience: for example, pulling into the gas station, filling up, checking the oil, paying the bill with a credit card, remembering to wash the windshield, and then driving away (did you remember to replace the gas cap?). While all this is going on, you are aware of details, the specific moves and gestures of even the simplest action. Each step and partial step in the process is clear and separate. But later, when you're walking the dog around the block and thinking about a logical problem in the paper you're writing, if you unexpectedly ask yourself whether you bought gas or not, the recollection fractures and blurs, some small aspects sharply focused, the others cloudy and vague. The coherence of the experience is gone forever.

the blue surrounded
by its attendant fragments
the E taken from
an *Elle* cover, a page torn
from a notebook's square collage

like experience
one thing effaces what was
before sharp and clear
now muddied in fog, ideas
fade and contort, drop from sight

small as they might be
messages can be garbled
before the sentence
is complete. Nothing is clear
not after much less before

3

Suggestibility, undaunted by fear of proving
foolish, is essential to art love.

—Peter Schjeldahl[3]

With a kind of love for contending forces and formations, the field of battle here between the artifacts and the steam seems to be a place of half-formations, of ideas that once uttered wrench themselves away, content with mere suggestion. The weightier of the structures hangs down to the left, the lighter flight-borne images, unfinished in any real sense, nevertheless can fly. Perhaps the smaller, more refined group chooses elements from the thicker, weightier batch and draws them over, lures them across for refinement. Then the pile of rough shape and color on the left must be raw material for the heavenly revisions undertaken on the right. There is an energy of struggle and contradiction and color here giving the painting life, like a coiled spring in a watch pushing forward millisecond by millisecond.

revisions of mood
give life to the day-by-day
there's only so much
to see, hear, and try to do
so go take another look

things we say we know
are made up, of course, of bits
and pieces. Splinters
we try to reassemble
giving the world coherence

but a sharp eye sees
not only what is seen, but
what was intended
and rushes away with it
a treasure spirited off

---

1. *Artifact With Steam* (mixed-media painting: acrylic, ink, collage, brown bag, monotype, watercolor on canvas; 36" x 48") by Ann Knickerbocker, whose blog and galleries are available online at: https://annknickerbocker.com/home.html

2. Quotation by Ann Knickerbocker is from her online gallery: https://annknickerbocker.com/artwork/4534741-Artifact-with-Steam.html

3. Peter Schjeldahl, "The Spectacle of the Spectacles" (*The New Yorker*, 4 June 2016); link was retrieved on 17 June 2019: https://www.newyorker.com/culture/culture-desk/the-spectacle-of-the-spectacles

✧

I. Modern Dance

*no messages here
but ones twirling to the music
describing dance's
essence, embodiments of
feeling inscribed in the air*

[…]

Dancing is about acting, about being a liar, basically. Because often you don't feel like dancing, but it's your job. So you get out there and you do the movement, and it's not happening. So you work harder, you work harder, you go deep inside what you're about.

—Dudley Williams, from "Leaving Ailey"
in *The New Yorker* Dance Department (May 2005)

✧

Alvin Ailey's *I Wanna Be Ready*

Movement never lies. It is a barometer telling the state of the soul's weather to all who can read it.

—Martha Graham[2]

1

The old man came slowly up the beach, reaching as far forward as he could with his right leg, hesitating, and then dragging the left leg forward, his boot plowing a long, narrow furrow in the sand. Right leg stepping out, left leg limp and shrunken, dragging itself level. His body had no other coordination. The arms flailed and flapped. His head twisted vehemently at the end of his neck. He bent forward, straightened up, and leaned to the right and then to the left. Behind him and then in front of him, off to either side, coming back and in front again, a little black dog scampered, never getting too far away from the old man who moved slowly along. The dog would come up close, bark its high-pitched halting bark, and then run back to the circling pattern, as if on a tether. The old man paid no attention to the dog, absorbed as he was in his strange dance up the beach.

take a graceful bird
an osprey; watch it diving
in the windy surf
snatching guilty Menhaden
that squirm in the devil's talons

death is reaching in
frightened souls writhing in fear
now God's promises
about to be tested. Oh!
I pray my truth's all been told

struggling with unseen
devils, hoping I haven't
sinned too much. Sing it!
low and moaning; make the church
tremble to the sounds of dread

2

When the confident choreographer was asked what the dance movements expressed, he showed us that with your feet apart and your knees slightly bent, it meant to display strength, and when you pushed your right arm out from your side, and then your left, it meant intimacy with the people all around you. Does that mean if you leaned forward and touched the floor, then you were saying you were part of the earth, but when you straightened up and reached overhead you were calling on God? A clenched fist, then? Rolling over several times and then leaping to your feet, your face contorted in a silent scream of (what?—rage?). The dancer moves on the outside, thinks or feels on the inside, but we don't have a suitable lexicon, so all the meaning (if there is meaning) in the moves remains forever private.

he translates feelings
with a wild kick and a roll
then changes his mind
calls it all *"force d'elegance"*
instead, his paean to beauty

none of these little
turns are quite routine
how we tie our shoes
reach thoughtlessly to open
the door, racing up the stairs

possibilities
of the human bones, how
they are connected
where they are hinged, where rigid
every limb goes its own way

3

The Highlander's football team lined up across from the Claremont College team; the Highlander's center was bent over the ball, and the quarterback was up close and hunched over him. The offensive backs were arranged in the split-T formation; the fullback, hands on his knees, stood a half-step behind his flanking halfbacks on either side. The quarterback shouted out the signals—*hut one, hut two, hut three!*—and the center snapped the ball into the quarterback's hands, who turned quickly hard to the right, just as the right half-back charged toward the line. The quarterback pretended to give him the ball, but pulled it back at the last moment, as the halfback charged past him and into the oncoming defenders. The quarterback then moved two steps along the backs of the linemen, and pitched the ball gracefully out to the fullback, who was coming around fast in a wider arc to the right, with the left halfback running interference. "It's a lot like ballet," Coach Selin used to say.

"get up off your back"
as if God were saying that
then knocking you down
every time you tried. Could you
fly in the face of the Lord?

if every movement
actually had a meaning
all its own, what would
all this twisting and turning
be saying—could we read it?

a black crow flew down
and hopped around the road kill
jumping in fury
as cars sped past disturbing
his cold ritual supper

1.   Still photograph of Matthew Rushing in *I Wanna Be Ready* at Jacob's Pillow in 2013, a video sample of which can be viewed online at: https://danceinteractive.jacobspillow.org/alvin-ailey-american-dance-theater/i-wanna-be-ready-from-revelations/

A longer version of *I Wanna Be Ready* (an African-American spiritual sung by a small choir, danced by Matthew Rushing, and filmed at Alvin Ailey's old childhood church in Rogers, Texas) can be viewed at: https://vimeo.com/262406894

2.   Quotation is from "An Athlete of God," an essay by Martha Graham first aired circa 1953 and reprinted in the Historical Archives of NPR dot org (4 January 2006); link was retrieved on 12 June 2019: https://www.npr.org/templates/story/story.php?storyId=5065006

✧

The Red Circle and the Blue Curtain

*…spontaneity—the notion that creativity
comes from a deep interior region…*
—Bill T. Jones[2]

1

In my political theory intro course in the theater building, we were
set to use dramatic improvisation to see what we might have
overlooked in our reading of Machiavelli's *Prince.* Each group of
three students picked a chapter from the book to then interpret with
small group movement. After each group went off to talk over what
they would do, the performances began. The first group had chosen
Chapter 12, on mercenary armies. The tallest of three students
walked slowly downstage to the apron, with the other two students
close on either side. He stopped and looked out to the audience.
Abruptly, the other two attacked him and he ran wildly away. The
second group chose chapter 7, intended for those new princes
dependent on *fortuna.* The three students formed a ring and circled,
faster and faster, until, one after another, they all fell down. The third
and last group had chosen Chapter 26, the "Exhortation to Liberate
Italy from the Barbarians." They huddled in the center of the stage,
paused, and then rushed away in different directions, waving their

arms in the air and crying out, *"O, Italia, prenderà l'arme, prenderà l'arme!"*

no messages here
but ones twirling to the music
describing dance's
essence, embodiments of
feeling inscribed in the air

words by convention
only mean something to us
because we've agreed
to call this an "apple," that "hope"
but don't just stand there and wave

dance to the music
and forget the sentences
oh, what a wild leap!
then he curled round on himself
sprung up: *Hochsprung mit Musik*

2

Bill T. Jones's performance *Analogy/Ambros: The Emigrant* was meant to present W. G. Sebald's long chapter "Ambros Adelwarth," from his novel, *The Emigrants*. Now, you don't have to think too hard about it to realize that dance doesn't exactly "mean" anything but itself. Jones's dancers rushed around the stage, ducked in and out of large panels, with doors and windows cut out of them, which some of the dancers lifted and twisted and turned in the air, while other dancers paired like a *chœur dansé* or leaped and turned and rolled gracefully on the floor. A strange kind of music, partly live and partly recorded, gave the dancing *un mannequin de couture* to hang and fit itself upon. Then there were voices coming over the speakers, and Jones was reading aloud from Sebald's book while a female voice was singing other less certain lyrics. We strained to hear what exactly was being said because it was all we had to give any definite "meaning" to the dancing.

a dance I thought up
also used cello and voice
but instead of Jones
dancing, Marques Haynes was dribbling
in circles round and around

Ambrose and Cosimo
dragged the hurt rags of their lives
all around the world
but were mainly disappointed
how nothing came up to snuff

> *Beyond the valley of Jehoshaphat, where at the end of time, it is
> said, the entire human race will gather in the flesh, the silent city
> rises from the white limestone with its domes, tower and ruins.*
>
> —*The Emigrants*[3]

with each stab of pain
we strengthen our conviction
that this cannot be
the real world. Something greater
must await us beyond life

3

The very idea of dance! "If you're not dead, then you're dancing," the
old man said. "You wake up, go out to the kitchen and make the
coffee—carefully—measuring in the water and the coffee and
turning on the burner." He swung his legs out from under the covers
and around to the floor and stood up. He walked purposefully,
setting out slowly and then speeding up, into the kitchen, reached up
for the coffee, down for the percolator, twisted the faucet and ran the
water in, turned and faced the stove, twisted the knob, and watched
patiently as the fire came up. He set the pot down on the fire, turned,
and walked, again with great purpose, back to the bedroom. Such
strange and mysterious movements. Was that Elvis on the radio?

what these graceful
gestures might possibly mean
you wake up and stretch—
an arm goes this way, a leg rolls
over as if to say—not yet

but you could make them
communicate an idea
with fingers and fists
meaning letters and numbers
or waving semaphore flags

his arm bent this way
right elbow tucked as he flies
past and lands rolling
O, God! It's so expressive!
what can it possibly mean?

---

1. Still photograph is from the improvised TED performance by dance choreographer Bill T. Jones, and TED Fellows Joshua Roman and Somi, which can be viewed at:
    https://www.ted.com/talks/bill_t_jones_the_dancer_the_singer_the_cellist_and_a_moment_of_creative_magic?language=en

2. Quotation is from "Bill T. Jones and two TED Fellows create a work of art…in two days" in *TED Blog*, How This Talk Came to Be (7 May 2015); link was retrieved on 12 June 2019:
    https://blog.ted.com/bill-t-jones-and-two-ted-fellows-create-a-work-of-art/

3. From *The Emigrants* by W. G. Sebald, as translated from the German by Michael Hulse (New York: New Directions, 1996), page 144.

✧

William Forsythe: *One Flat Thing, Reproduced*

1

A boy and a girl maneuver beside, over, and under a metal table, stretching, lifting, bending, kicking, twirling, leaping up and jumping down. They dance together; they dance apart. All around them are more tables, twenty in all, and more boys and girls, dancing around them, boys with boys, boys with girls, girls with girls, in such a variety of moves and gestures you cannot see them all at once. We know from analysis of moving pictures taken of the dance that it was not all chaos and improvisation; there were patterns suggested in what the dancers danced, there were hints of coordination, there were rhythms here and there counted off by the dancers themselves, clicking their tongues or shouting out loud. And the dancers walk away to the starting point, wait, and then come forward again eccentrically, first just one or two, then six, then five, then three... try to catch it all... well, you see what I mean.

the human body
pivoting past myriad
axis points, from knees
to shoulders, neck, and ankles
a marionette on strings

watching sapling limbs
in a strong wind, or breakers
crashing on the rocks
or plows turning over rows
of rolled-up furrow slices

as if someone tore
pages from a kid's flick book
and rearranged them
so a hand grabs for a wrist
but comes up with an ankle

2

As the audience was filing out of the theater, I overheard a woman just ahead of us ask her husband, "But, what does it mean?" I was thinking along the same lines. Sure, it was interesting, you might even say it was exciting, but was there any story, anything like an idea? Was it, maybe, the report of what modern life is about? A critique of the pace of urban existence? And were the dancers, when they leapt up on the tables and then sat down and slid across, and pointed their left foot upward, trying to signal "exaltation?" But what if other dancers were doing the same thing, but meant all the time to say "impatience," for example, then what? Wait, though, the choreographer must have intended certain emotions while designing and rehearsing the steps, but since he was not performing on stage, was not inside each body making the moves, does that even count?

not further mincing
words, these are an asylum's
inmates on the loose
each one disembodying
their unutterable truths

unless you're talking
about semaphore or sign
language, or a shrug
or a finger up to your eye
bodies really never speak

oh, what about when
his shoulders sag and his face
falls just before he
leaps in the air *en dedans*
singing "toot-toot tootsie, goodbye"?

3

Think of it as a classroom: the teacher is away, and the children are dancing and clowning around on the rows of desks, leaping over some, standing up on others, running around the room, posing and teasing and frolicking. They hear the clack-clack of the teacher's heels coming back, and they all rush to their seats and fold their hands on the desks. But it was a false alarm, and one boy jumps up on his desk and starts tap dancing. "Hey," he says, "look at me!" Another boy climbs up onto his desk and starts to run in place, stomping out some unheard rhythm in his head. "Look at me!" he shouts. "I'm a Yankee-Doodle Dandy." Everyone's slapping the desks and shouting, "Go! Go!" when the door opens, and the teacher walks in, looks around, and says, "So you think you can dance?" as she leaps up on her desk and begins a complicated ballet sequence while the children stare in rapture.

how close does dance come
to reiterating things
from the everyday?
do we imagine, but for
strict training, it could be us?

close your eyes and dream
of Teacher with no clothes on
there's more than one way
to disobey the rules. What
if we all danced all the time?

spontaneous dance
makes it so easy to say
where formal dancing
came from. Watch for tapping toes
someone wriggling on a bench

---

1.   Still photograph is from a sixteen-minute film of William Forsythe's *One Flat Thing, Reproduced* as performed by 14 dancers of the Forsythe Company, which can be viewed via this link (retrieved 15 June 2019): https://vimeo.com/41151136

✧

SEA: Streb Extreme Action

…I ask, how can movement elicit sorrow, fright, humor, excitement, and the desire to live a better life—all at once.

—Elizabeth Streb[2]

1

By some process of abstraction (or so it seemed to me) the choreographer imagined an animated geometry in Time, a very real but brief flying in the space-time continuum. The dancers shoot left and right from their trampoline across intersecting curving lines in Space and Time from A toward B, from C toward D, and then right into the audience's imagination. In the very idea of air, in the biomechanics of the projected, soaring, weighted body, in the algorithms of lift and duration, the idea of flight keeps humming.

in a room writing
poems, repeating things I heard
when the dancers spoke
about that point before they
fell heavily back to earth

any catapult
makes you picture weightlessness
thinking you can fly
a short threatening second
when anything could happen

hundreds of such seconds
disparate and unconnected
come together then—
in your imagination
you are a soaring eagle

2

So, now, here's a little truth from the other side: no matter how high you fly you have to come down. Even if your lust to fly is bigger than the sky itself, you will still have to come down. Imagine the greatest ever success at flying, whether you're a bird or a rocket or just a jumping man, sooner or later, you have to come down. This is simply physics, of course, but also psychology. When you try to fly, especially when you succeed, and you want so badly to stay up, you can't understand why you have to come down; but when you come down the truth is waiting for you and slams your body down against the earth.

though we strain against
gravity's chains, pushing up
just like Sisyphus
or Jack and Jill, we come tumbling
down to earth. It is one thing

to go up, but still
another not to come down
take a rocket ship
past the moon, go out beyond
the stars, flying weightlessly

there is still coming
down when the rocket plays out
at the galaxy's
edge, motor and inertia
winding down. We cannot fly

3

It was a mix of childhood conceits, the towel tied around my neck, the S imagined on my shirt, and the fantasy flying. I remember it now, closing my eyes and seeing myself fly in defiance of all limitation. On a Ferris wheel once, stopped at the zenith, the gondola gently rocking on its old, heavily greased iron bearings, I was both afraid of dying but indifferent to the leaden world below. If it ended here, this was a hell of a way to go, so I stood up and rocked the gondola more, knowing it would never fall off, but at the same time terrified it would. This was what the existential edge felt like, and right then I knew there was no going back.

we are bracketed
by dreams and reality
the greatest pleasures
lasting only a second
but the memories live on

events in our heads
we feel and remember what
we felt, and moments
when the body spoke to us
live on in habits

buffeted by winds
through nerve endings and thinking
to put self together
nothing holds still, it all goes
through the wringer

1. Still shot from Elizabeth Streb's *SEA: Singular Extreme Actions*, performed at Skidmore College, Saratoga Springs, New York (2–22 June 2019). A video, *Streb SEA Promo*, is available via the following link (retrieved on 5 July 2019):
   https://www.youtube.com/watch?v=umEp0zNvBDY

   Other videos of performances by Streb's company of "action-hero dancers" may be viewed via the links below (retrieved on 5 July 2019).

   In slo-mo: https://www.facebook.com/STREBSLAM/videos/streb-extreme-action/346879079201034/

   Rehearsal of *Ascension* at the STREB Lab for Action Mechanics in Brooklyn; in this clip, Streb talks about her radical ideas, exploring for example, "What is the iambic pentameter of action?":
   https://www.youtube.com/watch?v=DK4a3lrv3Q0

   One Extraordinary Day, visually stunning performances at a few of London's famous monuments, as part of the London 2012 Festival commissioned by the Mayor in the run up to the Olympics Games:
   https://www.youtube.com/watch?v=_zS2_gydyf8

2. Quotation by Elizabeth Streb, New York choreographer and founder of the dance company Streb Extreme Action and SLAM (the Streb Lab for Action Mechanics), is from her intro on the home page of her website (link was retrieved on 5 July 2019):
   http://streb.org/elizabeth-streb/

   See also the TED talk "My Quest to Defy Gravity and Fly," in which Streb talks about redefining our ideas about human flight, the importance of learning how to land, and her invention of impact techniques and machines that help us fly, proving that "action is for all of us":
   https://www.youtube.com/watch?v=dd1IeIHA0S8

You have to love dancing to stick to it. It gives nothing back, no manuscripts to store away, no paintings to show on walls and maybe hang in museums, no poems to be printed and sold, nothing but that single fleeting moment when you feel alive...

—Merce Cunningham, in his book
Changes: Notes on Choreography (1968)

✦

Et Encore Plus Heterotopia

*…a train is an extraordinary bundle of relations because it is
something through which one goes, it is also something by
means of which one can go from one point to another,
and then it is also something that goes by.*

—Michel Foucault[2]

1

You, me, and the train; the train, you, and me. I am not you and I am
not the train. I am only walking through the train, to the dining car,
perhaps, or back to my seat. The train is passing through Mullingar
on its way from Dublin to Sligo. You are a lorry driver stopped at a
crossing in Mullingar and watching as the train speeds by. You are in
a hurry and somewhat annoyed. I am having tea in the lounge car
and, looking out, I see you, but barely, because you are going past so
quickly. The dancer is curled up on the floor, his right arm reaches
out ahead, curls back under the small of his own back, then thrusts
suddenly out! The movements fade in memory as fast as they rise to
consciousness, a flow like a movie, there and gone, around the stage
like a Chinese dragon dragging its tail in a parade. Do you see me
looking out? Did you see me wave? I am sitting and having tea and
looking out at you, and waving. All the time I am moving from Dublin

toward Sligo. Dublin is sliding away, forgotten; Sligo is waiting. You are gone behind the moving trees, and it takes me just under a mile to finish my tea.

two venerable soldiers
riding on the train, side by side
remembering their
wartime comrades, wondering
where they are now, doing what?

when I was a child
I had a toy. When you blew
on it like a horn
a fat paper snake shot out
puffed up, for just a second

describe the dance's
penmanship, arms and legs write
in the air, across
the floor. There's no message, though
just the dancer and the dance

2

Here, on the near the side of the road, stands an old farmhouse, the very idea of a farmhouse somewhere in Vermont or Iowa, built to a simple design with a small front porch under an overhang. Over there, you can see in a clearing in the woods what might have begun as a stack of glass-enclosed cubes, that have been twisted into wild irregularity; defying gravity, poised midair like a leaping dolphin, it almost seems to move. The dancer approaches, turns in flight, describing unforeseen marks, faster than the human eye connects them up. He dances along a path that is so quickly taken up, it's already a memory, an ethereal scaffolding of unseen, unheard-of forms. The house of glass sometimes reflects the sunlight; other times you can see right through it.

vocabularies
from ballet inscribe common
experiences
you can read an *arabesque*
fouette or *cabriolé*

improvisation
and you see the stockinged feet
leap, and crossing each
a stutter of positions
the e.e. cummings of dance

we see things quicker
than we can hear them, think them
much quicker than that
know things hitherto unknown
grasp the nothing, all at once

3

The dance dissociates only on film, where each frame captures a portion and makes an illusion of movements we can number. Otherwise, there is only the fading memory of the dancer having moved, leaped, turned, dropped, and flown. Is there anything else whose components live and die in an instant, forever? All our improvisations, maybe, in speech or music, where words or notes and timing arise and dissipate in an instant forever. Make up the music as you go, as you make up the steps and leaps and the words that are being said, then, make the whole thing up. Why, it's exactly like an ordinary day, throughout which we improvise the whole way, dancing and talking and humming like crazy. Eating, drinking, walking, talking, making love—oh, you couldn't rehearse or learn any of it by heart. It all would die in your wooden, mechanical, memorized gestures. The truth is that the most carefully learned and rehearsed routine aims, always and finally, for the illusive, the extempore.

try and draw the dance
where the pictures will be wild
untraceably
no picture of anything
ethereal as architecture

he set out to sketch
the spontaneous movement's
choreography
rode the moment, unrehearsed
untraceable lines and squiggles

on the lake's edges
where white winter's winds blew up
something like a surf
the water piled upon itself
frozen sculptures of pure motion

---

1. Still photograph is from the performance *Heterotopia* by Eldad Ben Sasson—not to be confused with the more elaborate and famous production of *Heterotopia* by William Forsythe—the former of which can be viewed via this link (retrieved on 15 June 2019): https://vimeo.com/142496929

2. Quotation by Michel Foucault is from *Architecture/Mouvement/ Continuité*, October, 1984 ("Des Espace Autres," March 1967; translated by Jay Miskowiec); link was retrieved on 13 June 2019: http://web.mit.edu/allanmc/www/foucault1.pdf

✧

Variations on a Theme by Bill T. Jones

1

CARMODY: *I never had you figured for a dance man.*

BLIGHT: *You were distracted by my spindly legs.*

The big stage resembling a basketball court was subtly lit, and people were still slowly making their way to metal folding seats. In the center of the stage wooden girders were piled awkwardly, propped against each other, as if they were being stored or had been discarded. On the left side, a mic waited in shadows. Before long, a woman came out from the dark and sat before the mic. The lights went very dim and then came full up. The woman's singing came slowly to fill the room as a bevy of dancers appeared as if by magic, and began to frolic in full circles around and around the stage.

all expectant thus
we waited, watching dancers
circling, announcing
transport to another place
their springing an alphabet

each one's words written
cursive, made from large letters
scrawled by twisting bodies
arched in their exotic lexis
words torn from their reaching arms

like the aching sounds
of tongueless, mute suffering
silent leaps and falls
scratch desperate messages
in the sand like ghostly birds

2

CARMODY: *I have had the recurring dream of flying,
had it since I was a child.*

BLIGHT: *"Behold the birds of the heaven, that they
sow not, neither do they reap, nor gather..."*[2]

The music stopped and a silence fell like sheer shrouding over everything; air suddenly became substance, falling over and between the dancers, who hurried on, their feet scuffing across the floor, their leaps adding to the soundless weight beneath which the dance, now driven from within, kept on with increasing frenzy, with each higher jump staying longer in the air. We waited now only to see if they would fly, so, we didn't notice the tall black man, stripped to the waist, enter slowly from the left, strike a perfect fifth position, just before he ran to the pile of wooden girders and flew over them, turning to face the audience from his apex in the air and, having landed, walked slowly off.

birds will talk about
what it's really like to fly
up air so solid
it holds you high above clouds
where whole worlds become whispers

high in Balsam Fir's
green limbs, thick and reaching out
you could swing backwards
one below, to another branch
your world turning upside down

try to imagine
you're up in a pirouette
just spinning around
like an antique Duncan top
at the end of a long string

3

CARMODY: (melodiously) *Have you ever seen
the silver salmon's* grand jeté *over the weir?*

BLIGHT: *I don't really have to go there, do I?*

Gradually the number of dancers on the stage grew and the music came back, augmented now by recordings of urban sounds, the staccato of a marimba against the car horns on a city street. The dancers formed a whirling gyre in the center of the stage which gradually widened to the edges. Then the cyclone pattern collapsed, and the dancers formed into smaller groups of three or four, each group now inventing, it seemed, their own dance interpretation to the cacophony. Someone was passing out grammar-school musical instruments to the audience—tambourines, cymbals, silver triangles, and tin kazoos. To the final din of all that uncoordinated sound, the dancers hefted the wooden girders and carried them off. The stage was empty, but the noise went on.

dancing makes you dream
making up your own music
to the steps and bends
were you wishing for a trombone
at the height of your *Saut de Chat*?

making dances from
movements of everyday life
stepping out of cars
going up and down the stairs
hanging wet clothes on the line

banging wooden blocks
scraping on the *güiro* gourd
shaking the jingles
blowing plastic recorders
murmuring through the kazoo

---

1. Still photograph is by Paul B Goode, of Bill T. Jones/Arnie Zane Dance Company in performance of *Story/Time* at Cal Performances in February 2012. Pictured: Jennifer Nugent (forefront), Erick Montes, and Bill T. Jones (seated). Link was retrieved on 13 June 2019: https://live.stanford.edu/sites/default/files/press/Bill-T-Jones-StoryTime.JPG

    Goode's photograph also appears in a review by Claudia Bauer, "Bill T. Jones' *Story/Time*," in the *San Francisco Chronicle* (28 February 2012); link was retrieved on 13 June 2019 (scroll down to page 73 of the PDF): https://newyorklivearts.org/pdf/Bill T. Jones-Arnie Zane Company EPK_March15.pdf

2. "Behold the birds of the heaven..." Matthew 6:26, the New Testament

✧

Falling & Loving

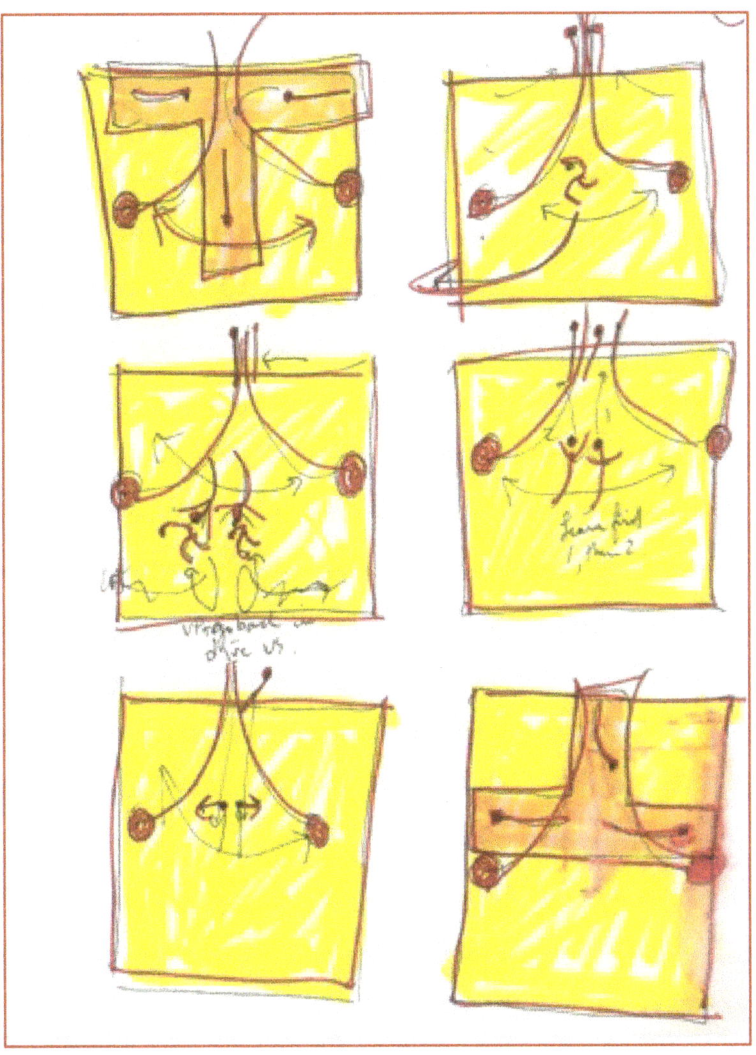

In other words, the personal "art coefficient" is like an arithmetical relation between the unexpressed but intended and the unintentionally expressed.

—Marcel Duchamp[2]

1

The old custodian came into the gymnasium as I was trying to figure out what all the contraptions were for, and I asked him if he knew. "I just sweep in here whenever some event is going to happen," he said. "What do you suppose these are for?" I asked again, pointing to the cords hanging down from the platform overhead. "The cords are fastened," he said, pointing up to the dozen or more little hoppers, "to those buckets up there and when they pull on the cords all sorts of material is going to fall." "Like what?" I asked. "Like confetti," he said, instinctively moving out of the way, "and peanuts, maple syrup, molasses, flour, milk, honey, sugar, popcorn, and mylar, they say." Two (or maybe there were three) bowling balls were hung on cables or ropes. He pushed one of them, like a tether ball, and it swung back and forth pendulum style. "I heard," he said, solemnly, "that the dancers have to dive and race through that little space at the perigee where the arcs of these swinging orbs threaten to intersect." "Timing would be everything," I added.

when an osprey drops
feet first from the sky, like a bomb
talons sharply out
the impact's ostentatious
rising phoenix with its prey[3]

danger as an art
requires us to savor fear
though dodging outcomes
at the very last minute
anyone can hit the wall

it is the moving
around confirms the human
kinesis as life
animals swim, fly, and run
even the trees hold on tight

2

Choreographers use many tools to create and record dances. The moves and gestures, arising out of the body's spontaneity or the brain's analysis, drift away like smoke as soon as they occur, unless some means is used to "record" them. One dancer creates moves as she goes, in thin air, and all we can do is rush to write or draw pictures of what we saw or record the motions in the codes of various dance notation systems.[4] Another dancer cogitates, imagines, and creates steps and motions, literally out of thin air, and writes them out for live dancers later to perform. The mystery of choreography resides, however, in questions about just how and why the dancer for the first time ever raised her right arm just so, then bent and twisted her torso in that way, or kicked high with her right leg…and just kept on going, pushing the dance in the imagination ahead of her while the dance already danced trailed behind in fading images, like the dragon at Chinese New Year.

drawings do provide
hints approximating dreams
choreographers
have about flying dancers
but they leave out the motion

you can only hint
with the use of curving lines
what you want to say
she flies on his outstretched arms
while escaping gravity

does his arm move first
or the image in his head
does he just know when
to start and stop or does he
wait to see it on paper?

3

Step back, now, and forget ideas of purpose or utility and consider the pictures above as pictures in their own right, as a work of art. Or, rather, see it as a composite work of art—drawings or a painting, on the one hand, made up of six abstract panels AND, at the same time, pushing past the idea of an inexplicit pattern of line, shape, and color, see it as a representation of an imagined dance. The dance abstracted, the abstraction dancing. What do you see when you peer deeply into a red and yellow window by Matisse, beyond the suggestion of some person, say, or the sea? You can't help but see the underlying geometry, the space and shapes, colors and arrangement. So, here, beyond the idea of dance motion, interaction, and time, is a yellow space, red lines, and stick figures, embodying the artist's multi-valenced urgency at the time.

say the hardest thing—
art is indeterminate
count off the factors
intention, form, genre, line
and color, just don't step back

too far, then things bleed
the edge into the center
a sympathetic
eye becomes a crude dollop
smudged with the edge of a thumb

imagination
finishes everything up
following the urge
from blurring gradually out
to the sharp "smack!" on the floor

1. Elizabeth Streb's *Choreographic Notes* for a new work in development by Streb and Anne Bogart, who were at Skidmore College in June 2019, to be performed by members of Streb Extreme Action and SITI Company. In June, Streb gave several pages of such notes to the author, Charles D. Tarlton, with kind permission to use them as he wishes.

   See the footnotes on page 31 for links to videos of SEA performances and Streb's TED Talk.

2. Quotation by Marcel Duchamp is from "Session on the Creative Act," a presentation at the Convention of the American Federation of Arts in Houston, Texas (April 1957), as published in *Marcel Duchamp* by Robert Lebel (New York: Paragraphic Books, 1959), pages 77 and 78: http://radicalart.info/things/readymade/duchamp/text.html

3. See the wonderful slo-mo short film of the Osprey's dance in water at: https://www.youtube.com/watch?v=yQOVcP67zFM

4. See Anna Heyward's useful essay, "How to Write a Dance," in the *Paris Review* (24 February 2015): https://www.theparisreview.org/blog/2015/02/04/how-to-write-a-dance/

   The three links above were retrieved on 6 July 2019.

The Architectural Dance of
Daniel Libeskind's *Micromegas*

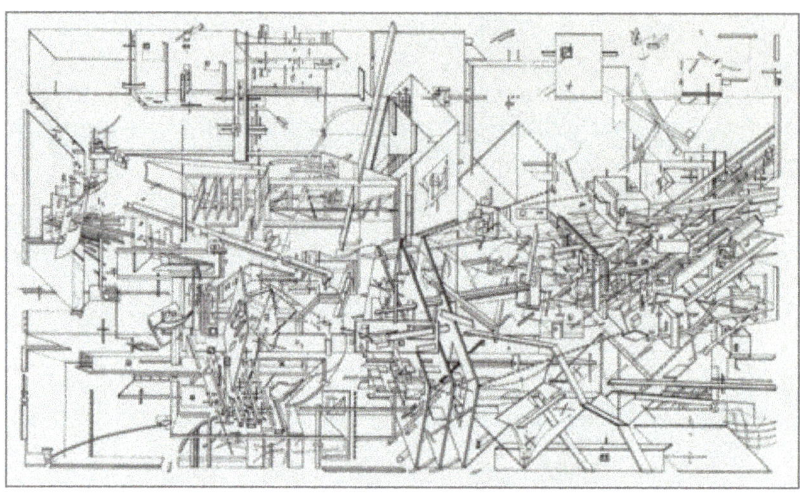

*"Well," said Micromégas, "maybe the inhabitants of this planet are
not of good sense! But in the end it looks like this may be for
a reason. Everything appears irregular to you here, you say,
because everything on Saturn and Jupiter is drawn in
straight lines. This might be the reason that you are
a bit puzzled here. Have I not told you that I have
continually noticed variety in my travels?"*

—Voltaire[2]

1

Somewhere beneath thought (malformed, vague, and wildly
iterated), in the moment when spoken words or made images give it
sound or physicality across a flattened page, somewhere, the idea
still bounces around. When the artist's hand scratches at the paper
or the stone with his tools (chisels and pens) and marks on it, what
would your first question be, if you were allowed to ask one? "Oh,"
someone says, "that's easy! Are they connected, I'd ask, that disarray
in your mind and the scratches your hand makes?" No design is ever
fully realized. Look, now, at the drawing above. At first it suggests a

plan or blueprint for something to be built, but looking closer you can see beams and cornices that begin and end nowhere. The connections that might make some whole are missing; there are only clues, hints, and suggestions, someone might say, false starts and the merest beginnings of going nowhere. Ideas start up, only to peter out, to be forgotten in the sense of a thought in two dimensions straining to be three. The line dances off the end of the pen; the line in materiality shows what the glimpse of an idea might be like— fractured, irregular, and insufficient.

this all ended up
in the inventory of disuse
your architecture
was empty. "You were making
models to the very end"

all architecture
remains allegorical
no design is ever
fully made. The idea of space
only between the broken lines

lines aping ideas
non-existent, shapeless, bland
behind whose pictures
of painted bowls, her smiling
eyes disappeared in a blur

2

A blue lamp was fastened to the male dancers' left wrists, red ones on their right wrists; then blue lamps to their right ankles, and red ones on their left. The overhead lights were switched off in the room and, as the guitarist and the singer began their song in the dark, the dancers ran across the stage, leaping high in the air. Some landed in a crouch, others rolled over on the floor, still others sprang in a twirling motion upwards, arms tightly wrapped around their chests, and then outstretched. The lights traced the moving spider web of thin red and blue contrails in the dark, twisting around one another like silk ribbons in the wind. The lines of light written in the darkness seem to have substance for a second, but, then, so quickly, they are only memories that remain of coiling red and blue creases, how they faded and went out like meteors or sparks rising from a fire.

dream architectures
become lawless, no line needs
end up anywhere
no idea begun, but runs
itself out, suddenly stops

waiting carries on
despite expecting it to
find its own limit
say, "go ahead, see what you
can do; stop when it seems right"

go dance the patterns
in a Persian rug, wallpaper
or the fireplace flames
how pens dance on the page
an architecture of sorts

3

There is a focus in formal art, whether poetry, painting, dance, music, or the plastic arts, a still place from which all the gestures originate and, as if from a catapult, pivot out into the fullness of the work. The resulting integrity and stability of form is something that artist and reader, listener and viewer can recognize and embrace, completing the circuit where artist's intention and viewer's expectation meld. But nothing lasts forever; it is inevitable that curiosity, impatience, envy, imagination, and perversity (most often among artists but also among spectators) arise to break with the established forms, wonder about something different, and see unexpected possibilities. Then the focus shifts. Expectations of resemblance, perspective, harmony, rhythm and rhyme, plot, action, and climax are overturned. The center shudders and gives way to energies from the periphery.

you can't help wonder
how they thought this one up, moves
so irregular
an elbow out, the leg up
quick, encircling, draws a line

each line of dialogue
stops mid-sense, the poetry
always hurrying
all the colors run headlong
musical phrases shatter

when it's always new
what's next is unexpected
keeps you interested
wide awake and sitting up
so, how did they think of that?

---

1. *Micromegas Project, Time Sections* (1979; silkscreen on paper, 26 x 36 1/8" [66 x 91.8 cm]) by Daniel Libeskind; drawing is held by the Museum of Modern Art (MOMA), Robert K. and Barbara J. Straus Family Foundation, Inc. Link was retrieved on 13 June 2019: https://www.moma.org/collection/works/295

2. Quotation is from *Micromégas*, the 1752 science fiction novella by French philosopher and satirist Voltaire (1694–1778).

✧

If a dancer dances—which is not the same as having theories
about dancing or wishing to dance or trying to dance
or remembering in his body someone else's dance—
but if the dancer *dances*, everything is there....

When I dance, it means: this is what I am doing.

—Merce Cunningham

from "The Impermanent Art" in
7 Arts: Number 3: Dance, Music, Theatre,
Painting, Sculpture, Literature, Architecture
(The Falcon's Wing Press, 1955), page 70

✧

Le Ballet des Freux

The cawing rooks whirl round the frosted stack,
Or crowd the dripping boughs....

—Oscar Wilde[2]

1

There are at least two possible theories of the origins of dance. In the first theory, dancing is *natural*, arising from the spontaneous expression of emotion. Here, the movements of arms and legs are like the furrowing of a brow, or the mouth twisted in agony. According to the second account, dancing is *artificial*, movements deliberately designed and eventually becoming part of an idiom or code, like the flag positions in classic semaphore. A third thing about dance is, however, that the most spontaneous and emotional routines can be learned and performed by another. When dancers today dance one of Isadora Duncan's wild prances in the surf, do they have to feel the same emotions as she did…is that even possible?

each rook rising
calls upon unconscious skills
not imagining
diving like a hurled stone
could turn itself into flight

as if the patterns
of their darts and curlicues
had been sketched before
on the air and they just went
where the lines told them to go

thrown handfuls of stars
diamonds or just common sand
sparkling in the sun
like a parliament of rooks
lifting as one from the trees

2

A bunch of us were eating lunch upstairs at Nieman-Marcus in San Francisco, and I turned from the conversation and saw out the window a hawk perched on the head of a gargoyle across the street. He was watching several flocks of pigeons as they flew back and forth down the canyon between the tall buildings. He seemed suddenly to just fall from his perch, as if he'd slipped off the gargoyle and fell, but then as he came closer to a passing flock of pigeons he put on the brakes, becoming suddenly an artful flier, and curved into the pigeons, feet and talons first. I saw a little silent explosion of feathers and, as the pigeons scattered in all directions, the hawk flew off with the one dead pigeon in his grip. He flew away over the tall buildings and disappeared.

not art but the real
thing, aerial dive bomber
doing loop-de-loops
as pigeons swim by like the slow
corps de ballet in *Black Swan*

the rooks really are
dancing, making pirouettes
as they turn to clouds
of black motion, shredding air
on their way back to the sky

I dream now of rooks
whenever I soar the night
skies. birds on sacred missions
little birds, mouths wide open
calling into the blackness

3

Libretto

At RISE: A large colony of rooks is returning to its familiar giant oak. The birds settle like black fruit on the still leafless branches. Restless, the rooks are eager to begin the task of nest building. We notice that they work in pairs as they first fly away and then come back with sticks and twigs in their beaks. In their pairs, they begin to push the sticks into the forks of high-up limbs, and after a time, a dozen large nests begin to take form. Still the rooks fly away, searching for more sticks and for food, and again they come straight back to the oak and to their mates. A scuffle breaks out in the highest nest; an interloper has tried to interfere with one of the rook couples. The pair drives him off. Birds continue to fly off again and come back. Flying up and settling down, they make a kind of dance up there in the branches, cawing and scuffling, bringing back more sticks, leaping in and out of the growing nests until, as the light dims and night arrives on the stage, the rooks circle slowly, find their places, and settle in. CURTAIN.

the rooks hoard wisdoms
they keep from the rest of us
and hardly notice
we're the crown of creation
just somewhere in the background

the world is dancing
everywhere the rhythms pulse
a dance of being
alive. Formal movement can't
keep up, can't twist quick enough

what a metaphor
for living, the rookery!
across the divide
there is something going on
you sense it, but can't get in

---

1.   Still photograph is from a video of rooks (*Corvus frugilegus*) dancing in and around a leafless tree, which can be viewed via this link (retrieved on 12 June 2019):
https://www.youtube.com/watch?v=IikaTbq-P_o

2.   Quotation is from the poem "Humanitad" by Oscar Wilde (1854–1900) in "Poems by Oscar Wilde; Also, His Lecture on the English Renaissance" (*The Seaside Library Daily*, Number 1183, 19 January 1862), page 26.

✧

II. Films

now get hold of this
there is of course a story
how dancing rises
above banality, tells
us the unspoken story

[...]

Annabelle Moore, née Annabella Whitford (1878–1961), was an American actress best known for her performances of the serpentine dance in a series of short films produced by Thomas Alva Edison:

Annabelle's Sun Dance (1894)

Annabelle's Serpentine Dance (1894 and 1895)

Butterfly Dance (1894, 1896, and 1897)

Tambourine Dance by Annabelle (1896)

Annabelle in Flag Dance (1896)

Sun Dance: Annabelle (1897)

A Mermaid Dance (1902)

✧

Annabelle Twirling (1897)

CARMODY: *This girl opens like a magic flower in a wind of changing colors.* (pause) *Don't you think?*

BLIGHT: *I couldn't hear a thing.*

1

We crossed the bridge from San Francisco to Berkeley to see Bill T. Jones's new choreography in a piece called *Story/Time.* Jones sat at a small table onstage, under a clock that counted down the seconds from 60 to 0, and read out one-minute-long stories in various styles, personal, political, philosophical. As he read a story, his dancers writhed and leaped and twirled and twisted and flew in a beautiful and fluid poem made of music and bodies. As the clock and story counted down to the end, those dancers moved off, and as he began to read a new story fresh dancers spilled onto the stage to create another painting in motion.

the dancers' movements
come all the way to the edge
of speech, inventing
their alternative to words
in the air with their bodies

it is not ballet
no remembered language here
it's all invented
as they go, as if learning
new letters for unheard sounds

dancing silently
no music, she makes her own
and we strain to hear
what the billowing fabric
says, what tune it is humming

2

Walt Disney's animated movie *Fantasia* includes a sequence, "The Dance of the Mirlitons,"[2] in which we first see widening and overlapping rings in the water of a pool where delicate flowers are floating down from the trees and into the water, pink flowers at first, then gold, and then blue. They turn and revolve in ballet unison to the music of Tchaikovsky's *Dance of the Reed Flutes*, metamorphosing into dancer-flowers as a large white blossom drops among them, and the dance revolves in ever larger circles into the center of the pool, gracefully round and round, and then gently over a bubbling little waterfall, with the white flower the last reluctantly to go.

she dances alone
the music and the story
just out of her reach
but the flowers have a life
all their own; she's living it

O, the dance circles!
endlessly, whirling upwards
down in another
outward circle, her sleeve ends
twirl into butterfly wings

she has been twirling
a century in silence
keeping the cosmic
rhythms that authenticate
the very idea of dance

3

If you were looking for the frontier between then and now, you could find it exactly where Turner's seas and Constable's clouds fail. They sought to capture on the stillness of canvas and in drying dollops of oil paint the vital movements of nature. The painter looks up and captures a vision of the moment and by the time he's turned back to the canvas, the moment has moved on. Yet, we stand in front of his picture and imagine we see the winds high up on a whiff of cloud like a tress of woman's hair, and need to wipe away the salt spray on our faces. But here with *Annabella* dancing, Thomas Alva Edison, in the most primitive of cinematography, and aiming for 46 frames per second, sped up the images of billowing silk till all we have to do is remind ourselves it isn't real.

turn it all around
pretend images reflect
the poems we've written
and let imagination
make me a picture of this

they might meet mid-air
colored, curling, flying silk
scarves about to speak
and words experimenting
with polished accents of silk

no art can subsist
in the absence of its tools
art remains outside
of us, a mediated
thing. Oh, right… there's singing

1.   Still photograph is from *Annabella*, one of several short films depicting the serpentine dance performed by Annabelle Moore and produced by Thomas Alva Edison (1847–1931) through the Edison Manufacturing Company in the late 19th century. The film (47 seconds long) can be viewed at the New York Public Library Digital Collections; link was retrieved on 16 June 2019:
https://digitalcollections.nypl.org/items/c23a0080-f875-0130-0759-3c075448cc4b

2.   The mirliton is a wooden flute-like instrument, now mainly for children. The Disney sequence may be viewed at:
https://www.youtube.com/watch?v=StvbtZfm-Jw

✧

An "Isadorable" Dancing in the Swash

The school of the ballet of today, vainly striving against the natural laws of gravitation or the natural will of the individual, and working in discord in its form and movement with the form and movement of nature, produces a sterile movement which gives no birth to future movements, but dies as it is made.

—Isadora Duncan[2]

1

The formalities of ballet, those forms and poses and steps, so like an alphabet for writing only one kind of story; they stick sometimes in the throat of a restless dancer. She feels bound around with ropes and chains, she can't find her breath, and when she has performed a perfect *arabesque* it seems as if she had just been reciting old familiar phrases, stale and dull. Oh, another might say to her that it was perfect! But that's just it, it's always perfect, but where's the risk, the adventure, and sense of novelty? If you know what's coming next, it tends to put you to sleep. The poet who counts the stresses per line, who rhymes *dance* with *romance*, and fits himself into the counted regularities of the *sestina*, fulfills the form, perhaps to perfection, but it is still only a form, like a triangle or circle, where knowing one or two parts, we then know all the rest. Who wouldn't want to step right out of the middle of that *double cabriolé*, and follow the arc of a deceiving elbow or ankle, wherever it goes?

his modern dancer
reins in her formalism
slides from her *penché*
twirls, curling up, and crouches
like a turbulent tiger

wild leaping salmon
going up the weir at Slane
push back on the Boyne—
here's one flying high; he twists
to a silver torpedo

a hurried plover
running *bourrée* over wetted sand
mad for tiny crabs
swerves first this way, and then that
in his choreography

2

Charles Olson wrote in his essay "Projective Verse" that the poetry of the future must follow no prescription "other than the one the poem under hand declares, for itself," and that that must be in the words as they are measured by the breath, and in a form that sticks to the subject at hand.[3] No more jamming thoughts and feelings into ready-made structures. And the writing principle is that no idea leads to anything but another and further idea. There is no looking back. In this vein, the dance, danced freely, leaps from one exhalation to another, as fast as the dancer's imagination (feeling) and feet can provide them. Each step sets up the next. The dancer-artist-poet finds that next move, the one that the preceding move requires, and from there goes on to the next, with no prior assumptions, certainly no formal story. Pound's lines in *The Cantos* spell out how "in the west mountain, Il Fiorentino,/ Seeing hell in his mirror," and then

shift quickly away to: "lo Sordels/ Looking on it in his shield;/ And
Augustine, gazing toward the invisible" (Canto XVI). The dancers run
and leap and run… O, follow it if you can!

does she know which leap
will be coming next? Will she
pirouette saltily
there in the sea, imagining
her companions in the surf

each dance step *gauche*
like a toddler's learning to walk
an aspiration
calling forth, carrying on
the dance of conceiving itself

a fact about rhythm
how melody and feelings
mix in the program
what an elevated kick!
follow it with something low

3

The dancer skipping her complicated poetry in kicks, jumps, and
poses in shallow water along the beach, her splashing counting, for
some, as expression—but expression of what? Consider the arbitrary
marks we think we understand, like the printed Alphabet, the
semaphore signal for E or 5, the letters and numerals in the Periodic
Table, the International Phonetic Alphabet, or what is more to the
subject here, complicated dance steps represented in any of the
dance notation systems that have been available for centuries.
Imagine sketches or stick-figures showing legs or arms rising and
falling, a reversal left-for-right, inscribed along a parallel musical
score. As your eyes follow the dancer now in the sea, rising and
falling, cavorting in the waves, imagine a little man behind her in the
water with a megaphone calling out to another man up on the sand a
succession of numbers or odd names of steps and gestures. See the

man up on the sand writing furiously on his clipboard—will anyone
ever remember? Go slower! What was she trying to exhibit as she
leapt and sprang (was there something crucial just before she raised
her right leg and both arms up in front of her?); what, in her heart,
was that movement satisfying, as the moment itself rushed past?

there's a thing we do
when we dance. Are we finding
possibilities
in the movement of our limbs?
are we imitating flight?

Yvonne de Carlo
hardening country bumpkins
as Salome, where
she danced, lithe as a cobra
Lester Horton's magic moves

or is it movement
to no purpose? Pointless leaps
savoring weightless
intoxication beyond
the sodden pull of gravity

1. *Anna Duncan at Long Beach* (photograph, 1917) by Arnold Genthe; very often mistaken as a photograph of Isadora Duncan herself. Anna Duncan was born Anna Denzler in Switzerland (lived 1894–1982) and was one of Isadora Duncan's "Isadorables," a group of her European students, all of whom were adopted by the dancer and went by her last name, Duncan. Photograph is reproduced here from the public domain via Wikimedia:
   https://commons.wikimedia.org/wiki/File:Anna-Duncan-danse-sur-la-plage.jpg

2. Quotation by Isadora Duncan (1878–1927) is from "The Dancer of the Future," in *The Art of the Dance* (New York; Theatre Arts Books, 1928):
   http://www.mccc.edu/pdf/vpa228/the dancer of the future - duncan.pdf

   Both links above were retrieved on 14 June 2019.

3. "Projective Verse" by Charles Olson in *Collected Prose*, edited by Donald Allen and Benjamin Friedlander (University of California Press, December 1997), reprinted at *Poetry Foundation* (October 2009); link retrieved on 25 August 2019:
   https://www.poetryfoundation.org/articles/69406/projective-verse

✧

*…sans tarder elle te livre à travers le voile dernier qui toujours reste, la nudité de tes concepts et silencieusement écrir ta vision à la façon d'un Signe, qu'elle est.**

—Stéphane Mallarmé,
in his essay *Ballets* (1886)

*Translated by Charles D. Tarlton as:

…without delay, she delivers unto you, across that last veil which always remains, the nudity of your concepts and silently writes your vision, like a Sign, which she is.

Alec Guinness and Yvonne de Carlo
Dance the Flamenco

Real flamenco is like sex.

—Klaus Kinski[2]

1

As a young man in high school, it always seemed madness to me that when it came to school dances all the normal rules were suspended. A boy could hold a girl's hand, he could put his arm around her, hold his cheek against hers, smell her hair, feel the touch of her body down to his knees. Your hand on the small of the girl's back, the tactility of her bra straps under her dress, and her soft whispering made you crazy. Breathless, you were unable to talk. And that's not even bringing up those dances where you were allowed to stand facing each other and move your legs and hips and hands mimicking sex as you imagined it.

not the story, no
but the dance that needs watching
who was he married
to when they did this cha-cha-cha?
see the way she works him up

belly-dancing, she
effused a vivid essence
filling the whole room
and stifling normal breathing
who knew you could move that way?

he'd heard that Yvonne
De Carlo just died of heart
failure. She'd caused his
heart to fail often enough
watching her heaving bosom

2

On the outskirts of Granada, in the summer of 1967, there was a Flamenco fair. The city had built row after row of temporary roofless tavernas on a vacant stretch of road just out of town, and in each one a small group of Flamenco guitar players, dancers, and singers stomped and clapped and snapped their fingers to the music. As we went from one taverna to the next, the tumultuous music from the last faded and then transformed into the music coming from the next. We found wine and dancing and singing everywhere, and I remember getting very drunk, and how the three of us, Bonnie, John, and I, ran loudly down the little street and into the night.

ecstatic mysteries
arose from the fierce music
pounding on the stones
sounds driving the dancers' blood
everyone beside themselves

a public display
this particular kind of dance
pushes up, reveals
bodies caught in relentless
darkly resonant turmoil

noises her shoes made
pounding the floor, *clack, clack, clack*
the scent of her sweat
violence strummed on guitars
El querer es cuesta arriba…

3

On one particular website I counted 110 guitar works by Picasso. They run the gamut of Modernist styles—from cubist paintings, burlap constructions, to twisted and distorted profile renditions in which you can make out only here and there some facet of a human form and the neck, body, and sound hole of a guitar. One picture, however, conventionally depicts a human: *The Old Guitarist* (1903–1904) shows an old man bent uncomfortably over a guitar. It is a picture full of pathos and sad beauty, but, as in all the guitar paintings, there is no music. They all are dead guitars, caricatured and distorted. When Yvonne de Carlo dances with Alec Guinness there is music from all sides, but no sound, no imaginations of sounds, not even the erasures of sound are found in any of Picasso's guitars.

sounds need vibration
to move the air, bouncing off
our eardrums making
us imagine we hear music
but the air on the canvas

cannot move. It's stuck
one long note in ennui
long since slowly silenced
by layers of drying paint
more and more faintly dying

perhaps we should first
watch and listen to the film
then turn from Yvonne
and dive into Picasso's strings
movie music in our ears

---

1. Still photograph above of Yvonne de Carlo and Alec Guinness, in mid-flamenco, is from *Captain's Paradise*, a scene which can be viewed at:
    https://www.youtube.com/watch?v=Ps3LNI0CvKg

    Watch them tango in this scene from the same movie:
    https://www.youtube.com/watch?v=Ps3LNI0CvKg&t=122s

    Both links above were retrieved on 16 June 2019.

2. Quotation is from *Kinski Uncut: The Autobiography of Klaus Kinski* (Penguin Books, 1997), page 179: "The flamenco of the Gypsy has nothing to do with the flamenco for tourists. Real flamenco is like sex."

✧

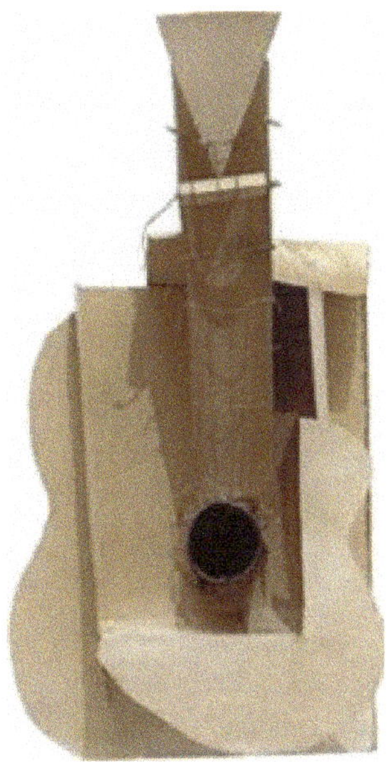

Above, left: *The Old Guitarist* (oil on panel, 1903-04) by Pablo Picasso is held by the Art Institute of Chicago and is reproduced here from the public domain via Wikipedia (link retrieved on 16 June 2019):
https://en.wikipedia.org/wiki/File:Old_guitarist_chicago.jpg

Above right: An image of *Guitar*, an assemblage, from *Picasso* (Paris, chez Delamain, Boutelleau et Cie, Librairie Stock), a small book by poet, artist, and writer Jean Cocteau containing 14 artworks by Picasso, which entered the public domain on January first, 2019. Reproduced here via *The Art Story Blog* (link retrieved on 16 June 2019):
https://www.theartstory.org/blog/picasso-works-entering-the-public-domain-in-2019/

✧

Bob Fosse and Tommy Rall: "The Alley Dance"
From *My Sister Eileen* (1955)

Choreography is writing on your feet.
—Bob Fosse[2]

1

Movie musicals present a dreamy and miraculous view of life, because in them murder and miracles, happiness and sadness are not just moments that come and go, but occasions for the characters to step out of the plot—and dance! Whole city streets of pedestrians and trolley drivers turn into singing, dancing choruses egging the heroes on, and promising them the moon. A quiet, horse-clop-clopping street from a Western becomes rows of tap-dancing cowboys, saloon girls, and bartenders. The cameras dolly down the dusty street following the boys and girls as they waltz and sing love songs. Teenage gangs, cynical carnival roustabouts, soldiers and sailors, gamblers, gangsters, hustlers, barbers, has-been actresses, Shakespearian noblemen, debonair bachelors and spoiled heiresses, trappers, nurses, and mountain men step away from their narrative scripts and start dancing.

what does the dancer
mean? There is no lexicon
or phrasebook for dance
oh, a high perfect scissors
might express exuberance

but it also could
suggest arrogance, so
what if we had said
the high scissors kick's a thing
and take it for what it's worth

dancing transports us
somewhere else, to places where
talk stops. Wave your arms!
when that's all that's left to say
just start kicking up a fuss

2

Bob Fosse's duet routine has its own vocabulary of slumps and glides, pirouettes and *arabesques*, hat-tricks and gestural tiptoe sliding, almost a mime. Fosse puts Tommy Rall through his vaudevillian paces. But, in the give and take of challenge and response, Rall, in turn, tests Fosse's ballet moves. They duel with styles, teasing, copying, taunting, and testing. Fancy jazz dancing versus classical ballet. Here's the thing, though, you could easily get lost watching this, and imagine two real prospective romancers representing two different conceptions of dance, competing for the same girl, each exploiting his own strength. But, you'd be wrong; Fosse dreamed the whole thing up, put in all the jivey bits as well as the *grand jetés*. The testing is fictional, a choreography in which Fosse lets both dancers do everything well.

taking the measure
of each other, great dancers
stretch the boundaries
how far, how high, can you
keep everything together

the hats are crucial
like Ginger with Fred Astaire
allowing themselves
to be put through their paces
making the dancers look good

watching dance duets
the critical eye looks out
for discrepancies
Rall, as Jacques d'Amboise recalls
could do triple spins for fun[3]

3

Only once did Fred Astaire and Gene Kelly dance together in a film and that was their comic tap-dance routine in George Gershwin's "The Babbitt and the Bromide," from the movie *Ziegfeld Follies* (1946).[4] The dance is mostly made up of the two of them tapping and doing Astaire-type moves through a tap-dance sampler of sorts, with a lot of broad humor and clowning thrown in. But, without our ever knowing exactly what's behind it, the implicit narrative anticipates the rivalry between Fosse and Rall above. The two dancers mirror each other through a dazzling array of recognizable maneuvers—tapping, spinning, and kicking in unison until both characters die and the dance moves to just outside the pearly gates. Wonderful to watch two dance "geniuses" working perfectly side by side, step for step, gesture for gesture.

now get hold of this
there is of course a story
how dancing rises
above banality, tells
us the unspoken story

of the truth behind
social formality, set
modes of intercourse
dancing tests categories
what's going on inside us

you can't dance alone
there's always you and the thought
of you alongside
here's a tricky step. do that!
piece of cake! what's the matter?

---

1. Still photograph of Bob Fosse and Tommy Rall is from the "Competition Dance" sequence of the musical *My Sister Eileen.* Video of the entire number can be viewed online via this link (retrieved on 15 June 2019): https://www.youtube.com/watch?v=ULuqdqxuDek

2. The quotation is from "Except for Bob Fosse" by Lionel Chetwynd in *Penthouse* (January 1974), page 91, as referenced in Chapter 5 ("Rhythm of Life") of *Big Deal: Bob Fosse and Dance in the American Musical* by Kevin Winkler (Oxford University Press, 2018).

[footnotes continued, next page]

3. "Jacques d'Amboise, the top male dancer at Balanchine's New York City Ballet, was wooed to Hollywood to play a brother in *Seven Brides for Seven Brothers*. Later, D'Amboise remembered working with Rall: during a break in filming, the dancers were talking about various moves and trying some things out. They agreed that the triple turn (spinning three times in the air) was incredibly difficult and they had only heard of a few people being able to do it.

"Well, Tommy Rall quietly stood up, did a triple turn, and sat back down again. D'Amboise (remember, he was a principal dancer at New York City Ballet) said he was absolutely stunned. So when you watch Rall spin in this dance, just take a moment to remember how difficult it is, because it looks like the easiest thing in the world when he does it!"

From the extended review of *My Sister Eileen*, by *The Blonde at the Film: A Fresh Look at Old Films*:
https://theblondeatthefilm.com/2014/05/13/my-sister-eileen-1955/

4. Watch Fred Astaire and Gene Kelly online:
https://www.youtube.com/watch?v=c1GV5o5xNqU

Both links on this page were retrieved on 15 June 2019.

✧

"Begin the Beguine": *Broadway Melody of 1940*

And even the palms seem to be swaying....

— Cole Porter[2]

1

The feet these people dance upon are magical; just watch them fly. Nimbly in their tapping shoes, they slide, jump, rattle, drum, and skip. Fred and Eleanor, matching each other twitch and wiggle for twitch and wiggle: they pull apart to really tap, and reach for the gestures each uniquely does, and then extend beyond their limits to do more. When you tap-dance, the way these terpsichorean gods and goddesses did, you defy the laws of physics and gravity and bend the charm of music to the needs of your pounding slippers. In another movie altogether, you can see Eleanor toe-tapping messages in Morse Code to a curious Red Skelton, and in another, Fred, inspired by love, tap-dancing up a wall and across the ceiling.

for which an empty
shoe cries out, a metal plate
for banging on the floor
trains your toes and ankles so
they move exactly quickly

little girls and boys
scraping, heel, toe, brush and drag
keep getting better
till they can move so quickly
eyes and ears can't see or hear it

who's best at tapping
making lists, rattling off names
do the chug and pop
can't always tell who's following
and no one looks at their feet

2

Fred Astaire danced with many different partners in the movies—his sister Adele, to start with, and then, in no particular order, Rita Hayworth, Judy Garland, Vera-Ellen, Joan Crawford, Cyd Charissse, Ginger Rogers—but he met his match in Eleanor Powell. While the others had all been actresses primarily (he had to teach Ginger Rogers how to tap-dance[3]), Eleanor Powell was a dancer all the way, first, last, and always. Besides, he could hardly spare the time to teach her; he was too busy keeping up. To look at this another way: they were equals dance-wise, Eleanor and Fred, and so you see them mainly dancing side by side, matching step and turn for step and turn, rat-a-tat-tat footwork for rat-a-tat-tat, gesture for gesture, alongside each other and not wrapped in each other's arms. They're more like girl-and-girl or boy-and-boy, than boy-and-girl. He tries hard to look straight ahead and not at her.

tap-dancing but so
competitive! Match that if
you can! He steps out
performs the impossible
she does it even quicker

like call and response
he taps it out, rat-a-tat
she follows him there
differently, tat-a-rat-tat
does a quick twist at the end

so often with Fred
in the movies, the women
seem accessory
I see him twirling one out
sweeping another back in

3

An interesting question: what is the relation between life, in general a matter of movement with purpose, and dancing? A man and a woman sit and talk on a park bench, and when the music comes up, they start dancing. Do we assume dancing is an extension of life in general, but involving different movements (ornate and complicated) and bewildering purposes? We watch intently in hopes of grasping what the dancing means, but in the end it only means what we can see—the reach and possibilities of the human body alive and, in addition, motions that are at the same time deliberate but lacking in purpose.

they lean in and tap
oh, the chance that was wasted
their strange messages
each body trying to talk
just where the words have run out

I'm talking to you
phrases fail me. So I reach
for my dancing shoes
put my body through baffling
moves, tapping out messages

the shape of the dance
will always be
how absent letters
forced the twirling and jumping
dumb mouths chewing down the words

1.   Still photograph of Eleanor Powell and Fred Astaire is from the dance sequence of "Begin the Beguine" in *Broadway Melody of 1940*, considered by many to be one of the greatest tap sequences in film history. It can be viewed online in its entirety (11 minutes) via the following link (retrieved on 15 June 2019); Powell and Astaire are joined by George Murphy during the final minute of the video: https://vimeo.com/104196921

2.   The line by Cole Porter is from the lyrics to "Begin the Beguine."

3.   "Ginger had never danced with a partner before [*Flying Down to Rio*]. She faked it an awful lot. She couldn't tap and she couldn't do this and that…but Ginger had style and talent and improved as she went along. She got so that after a while everyone else who danced with me looked wrong" (Fred Astaire, quoted in *Astaire: The Definitive Biography* [Hutchinson, 1987; page 127] by Tim Satchell).

✧

End Notes

The only way to know the truth
of a movement is to do it on your own body.

—Twyla Tharp, in her autobiography
Push Comes to Shove (Bantam, 1992)

Ich würde nur an einen Gott glauben,
*der zu tanzen verstünde.**

—Friedrich Nietzsche, in
Also Sprach Zarathustra (1885)

(Isadora Duncan called Nietzsche the first dancing philosopher.)

*Translated by Clare MacQueen as:

I would only believe in a God
who understood how to dance.

Contributor Bios

Charles D. Tarlton holds a Ph.D. in political philosophy/American history from UCLA and is a retired university professor of political theory who lives in Massachusetts with his wife, Ann Knickerbocker, an abstract painter. After retiring in 2006, he began writing poetry and flash fiction. His work has appeared in a number of print and online venues, including *Abramalin, Atlas Poetica, Barnwood, Blue and Yellow Dog, Contemporary Haibun Online, Cricket Online Review, Haibun Today, Houston Literary Review, Inner Art Journal, KYSO Flash, Linden Avenue Literary Journal, Peacock Journal, Prune Juice, Rattle, Red Booth Review, Shot Glass, Six-Minute Magazine, Skylark*, and *Ink, Sweat & Tears*, among others. He is also the author of these works:

(Photographer unknown)

1. *Touching Fire: New and Selected Ekphrastic Prosimetra* (KYSO Flash Press, 2018), a unique collection of more than 50 hybrid prose/poetry works created in response to fine artworks, 47 of which appear in full color in the book: http://www.kysoflash.com/Books.aspx#Fire

2. *Una Vida de Piedra y de Palabra* (twelve improvisations on Pablo Neruda's *The Heights of Macchu Picchu*), Number 23 in the 2River Chapbook Series, which features the author reading three sections aloud (II: Truth in the Larger Sense; IV: On Death, and Dying's Threshold; and XII: *Ecce Homo*):
http://www.2river.org/chapbooks/tarlton/default.html

   Chapbook also is available in PDF, with cover art by Ann Knickerbocker:
http://www.2river.org/chapbooks/tarlton/book/tarlton.pdf

3. "The Turn of Art," a short drama composed in verse and prose which pits Picasso against Matisse, in *Fiction International* (Issue 45, Fall 2012):
https://fictioninternational.sdsu.edu/wordpress/catalog/issue-45-about-seeing/

4. "Episodes in the Navajo Degradation: A Five-Poem Sequence" in *Lacuna: A Journal of Historical Fiction* (15 April 2012): http://lacunajournal.blogspot.com/2012/04/episodes-in-navajo-degradation-five.html

5. "*Five Lines Down*: An Interesting Moment in the History of Tanka in English" in *Atlas Poetica* (Issue 12, Summer 2012), pages 59-70. This analytical essay focuses on the seminal tanka journal of the 1990s, which published only four issues. Tarlton dives "deep into the poetry and essays of the short-lived journal, [and] urges us to give up the clichéd, sentimental, and obvious in favor of deeper truths, originality, and the unique assets of the English language" (M. Kei, *Atlas Poetica,* Issue 12; quoted here with his permission): http://www.atlaspoetica.org/wp-content/uploads/2019/05/12-Atlas-Poetica-Journal-of-World-Tanka-poetry.pdf

Ann Knickerbocker is an abstract painter who has shown her work in New England and on the West Coast and overseas; she has been a member of several galleries in Amherst, Massachusetts; Essex and Guilford, Connecticut; and Point Reyes Station, California (Gallery Route One). She also holds an advanced degree in literature. For links to her galleries and blog, *Artist in an A-frame*, please visit her website: http://www.annknickerbocker.com

Clare MacQueen served as webmaster and copy editor for 18 issues of *Serving House Journal* from its launch online in 2010 to its retirement in 2018. She co-edited *Steve Kowit: This Unspeakably Marvelous Life* (Serving House Books, 2015). She's also co-editor, webmaster, and publisher of *KYSO Flash*, the online literary journal she created in 2014 to celebrate a smorgasbord of short-form writings and visual art. Via KYSO Flash Press, she has produced 16 books, including anthologies and collections for writers and artists whose works have appeared in *KYSO Flash* online. Her own essays, reviews, stories, and poems have been published in *Best New Writing 2007, New Flash Fiction Review, Ribbons, Serving House Journal, Skylark, Winter Tales II: Women on the Art of Aging*, and elsewhere.

✧

Credits

Footnotes and annotations within this book were compiled by the publisher, Clare MacQueen, with kind assistance from the author, Charles D. Tarlton.

"Alvin Ailey's *I Wanna Be Ready*" was first published in *Contemporary Haibun Online* (July 2019, Volume 15, Number 2). All other prosimetric works herein were first published in *KYSO Flash* online (Issue 12, Summer 2019).

Visual images: Two of Pablo Picasso's artworks are reproduced on page 71 under United States public-domain license (PD-1923). Additional information about other images follows:

> **Front and Back Cover and Page 9:** Ann Knickerbocker's painting, *Artifact With Steam*, is reproduced with her permission. Copyrighted © 2019 by the artist. All rights reserved.

> **Title page:** *Dancing Sculpture* [unable to determine artist's name], a photograph by "Ralphman" depicting a "metal sculpture dancing her way across the Marin County sky at the Sausalito Art Festival" (2 September 2006), is reproduced here from Flickr under license, Attribution-ShareAlike 2.0 Generic (CC BY-SA 2.0):
> https://creativecommons.org/licenses/by-sa/2.0/legalcode

> **Page 83:** Photograph of the author is by an unknown photographer and is reproduced with Tarlton's permission. All rights reserved.

> **Back Cover and Page 86:** The KYSO Flash logo is copyrighted © 2015 by Clare MacQueen and was designed in collaboration with James Fancher. All rights reserved.

Permissions: Except for short quotations within critical articles or reviews, no portion of this book (including its covers) may be used, reproduced, or transmitted in any form or by any means, electronic or mechanical, including photocopying, or by any information storage or retrieval system, without permission in writing from the individual copyright holders.

✧ ✧ ✧

All web addresses herein were tested and found valid in
August 2019, a few weeks before this book's release.

KYS/O
Flash
www.kysoflash.com

an online literary journal &
a micro-press of printed books

Knock-Your-Socks-Off Art and Literature